Route

Printed in the United States of America

The Publisher: Wandering Walks of Wonder Publishing

Kansas City, MO 64118

USA

Website: www.wanderingwalksofwonder.com

ISBN-13: 978-1512074574

ISBN-10: 1512074578

This Journal

Belongs to:

____

U.S. Route 66 (US 66 or Route 66), also known as the Will Rogers Highway and colloquially known as the Main Street of America or the Mother Road, was one of the original highways within the U.S. Highway System. Route 66 was established on November 11, 1926, with road signs erected the following year. The highway, which became one of the most famous roads in America, originally ran from Chicago, Illinois, through Missouri, Kansas, Oklahoma, Texas, New Mexico, and Arizona before ending at Santa Monica, California, covering a total of 2,448 miles. It was recognized in popular culture by both the hit song "(Get Your Kicks on) Route 66" and the Route 66 television show in the 1960s.

Route 66 served as a major path for those who migrated west, especially during the Dust Bowl of the 1930s, and it supported the economies of the communities through which the road passed.

As you travel Route 66 I hope this journal gives you the opportunity to pause and reflect on the history of not only Route 66 – but the history of America itself.

Happy Travels!

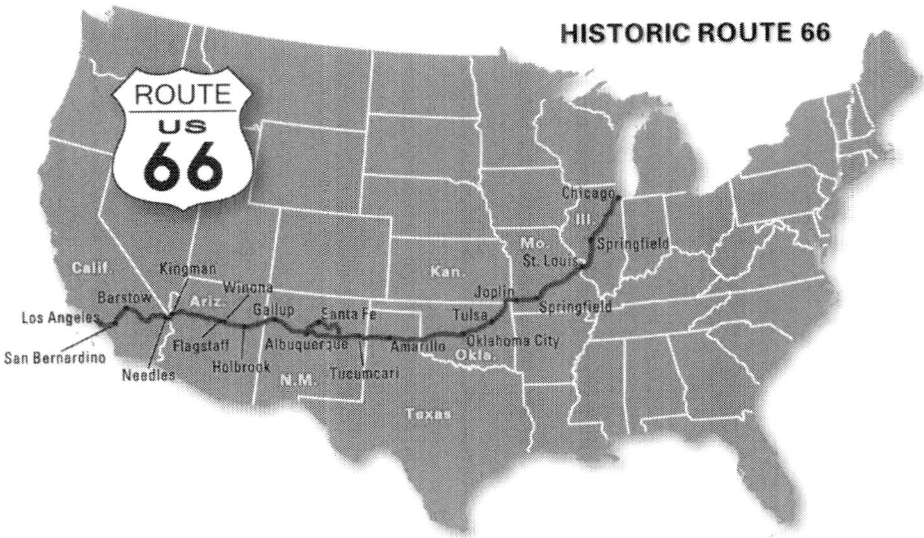
HISTORIC ROUTE 66
ROUTE
US
66
Chicago
Ill.
Springfield
Mo.
St. Louis
Kan.
Joplin
Springfield
Tulsa
Oklahoma City
Okla.
Amarillo
Texas
Tucumcari
Santa Fe
Albuquerque
N.M.
Gallup
Holbrook
Winona
Flagstaff
Ariz.
Kingman
Needles
Calif.
Barstow
Los Angeles
San Bernardino

Date:	Starting From: Destination::	Miles Driven:
Weather:	Cities and Towns I saw:	People I met:

Reflections on the Road Today:

Major Sites Today:

Other places visited, restaurants, where I stayed:

Date:	Starting From: Destination::	Miles Driven:
Weather:	Cities and Towns I saw:	People I met:

Reflections on the Road Today:

Major Sites Today:

Other places visited, restaurants, where I stayed:

Date:	Starting From: Destination::	Miles Driven:
Weather: ☼ ⛅ 🌧 🌨	Cities and Towns I saw:	People I met:

Reflections on the Road Today:

Major Sites Today:

Other places visited, restaurants, where I stayed:

Date:	Starting From: Destination::	Miles Driven:
Weather:	Cities and Towns I saw:	People I met:

Reflections on the Road Today:

Major Sites Today:

Other places visited, restaurants, where I stayed:

Date:	Starting From: Destination::	Miles Driven:
Weather:	Cities and Towns I saw:	People I met:

Reflections on the Road Today:

Major Sites Today:

Other places visited, restaurants, where I stayed:

Date:	Starting From: Destination::	Miles Driven:
Weather:	Cities and Towns I saw:	People I met:

Reflections on the Road Today:

Major Sites Today:

Other places visited, restaurants, where I stayed:

Date:	Starting From: Destination::	Miles Driven:
Weather:	Cities and Towns I saw:	People I met:

Reflections on the Road Today:

Major Sites Today:

Other places visited, restaurants, where I stayed:

Date:	Starting From: Destination::	Miles Driven:
Weather: ☼ ⛅ 🌧 🌨	Cities and Towns I saw:	People I met:

Reflections on the Road Today:

Major Sites Today:

Other places visited, restaurants, where I stayed:

Date:	Starting From: Destination::	Miles Driven:
Weather:	Cities and Towns I saw:	People I met:

Reflections on the Road Today:

Major Sites Today:

Other places visited, restaurants, where I stayed:

Date:	Starting From: Destination::	Miles Driven:
Weather:	Cities and Towns I saw:	People I met:

Reflections on the Road Today:

Major Sites Today:

Other places visited, restaurants, where I stayed:

Date:	Starting From: Destination::	Miles Driven:
Weather: ☼ ⛅ 🌧 🌨	Cities and Towns I saw:	People I met:

Reflections on the Road Today:

Major Sites Today:

Other places visited, restaurants, where I stayed:

Date:	Starting From: Destination::	Miles Driven:
Weather:	Cities and Towns I saw:	People I met:

Reflections on the Road Today:

Major Sites Today:

Other places visited, restaurants, where I stayed:

Date:	Starting From: Destination::	Miles Driven:
Weather:	Cities and Towns I saw:	People I met:

Reflections on the Road Today:

Major Sites Today:

Other places visited, restaurants, where I stayed:

Date:	Starting From: Destination::	Miles Driven:
Weather:	Cities and Towns I saw:	People I met:

Reflections on the Road Today:

Major Sites Today:

Other places visited, restaurants, where I stayed:

Date:	Starting From: Destination::	Miles Driven:
Weather:	Cities and Towns I saw:	People I met:

Reflections on the Road Today:

Major Sites Today:

Other places visited, restaurants, where I stayed:

Date:	Starting From: Destination::	Miles Driven:
Weather:	Cities and Towns I saw:	People I met:

Reflections on the Road Today:

Major Sites Today:

Other places visited, restaurants, where I stayed:

Date:	Starting From: Destination::	Miles Driven:
Weather:	Cities and Towns I saw:	People I met:

Reflections on the Road Today:

Major Sites Today:

Other places visited, restaurants, where I stayed:

Date:	Starting From: Destination::	Miles Driven:
Weather:	Cities and Towns I saw:	People I met:

Reflections on the Road Today:

Major Sites Today:

Other places visited, restaurants, where I stayed:

Date:	Starting From: Destination::	Miles Driven:
Weather:	Cities and Towns I saw:	People I met:

Reflections on the Road Today:

Major Sites Today:

Other places visited, restaurants, where I stayed:

Date:	Starting From: Destination::	Miles Driven:
Weather: ☼ ⛅ 🌧 🌨	Cities and Towns I saw:	People I met:

Reflections on the Road Today:

Major Sites Today:

Other places visited, restaurants, where I stayed:

Date:	Starting From: Destination::	Miles Driven:
Weather:	Cities and Towns I saw:	People I met:

Reflections on the Road Today:

Major Sites Today:

Other places visited, restaurants, where I stayed:

Date:	Starting From: Destination::	Miles Driven:
Weather:	Cities and Towns I saw:	People I met:

Reflections on the Road Today:

Major Sites Today:

Other places visited, restaurants, where I stayed:

Date:	Starting From: Destination::	Miles Driven:
Weather: 	Cities and Towns I saw:	People I met:

Reflections on the Road Today:

Major Sites Today:

Other places visited, restaurants, where I stayed:

Date:	Starting From: Destination::	Miles Driven:
Weather:	Cities and Towns I saw:	People I met:

Reflections on the Road Today:

Major Sites Today:

Other places visited, restaurants, where I stayed:

Date:	Starting From: Destination::	Miles Driven:
Weather:	Cities and Towns I saw:	People I met:

Reflections on the Road Today:

Major Sites Today:

Other places visited, restaurants, where I stayed:

Date:	Starting From: Destination::	Miles Driven:
Weather:	Cities and Towns I saw:	People I met:

Reflections on the Road Today:

Major Sites Today:

Other places visited, restaurants, where I stayed:

Date:	Starting From: Destination::	Miles Driven:
Weather:	Cities and Towns I saw:	People I met:

Reflections on the Road Today:

Major Sites Today:

Other places visited, restaurants, where I stayed:

Date:	Starting From: Destination::	Miles Driven:
Weather:	Cities and Towns I saw:	People I met:

Reflections on the Road Today:

Major Sites Today:

Other places visited, restaurants, where I stayed:

If you enjoyed this journal, we have many more styles and types to choose from. Visit our website for a complete list of journals.

www.wanderingwalksofwonder.com

Baseball Stadium Exploration Journal

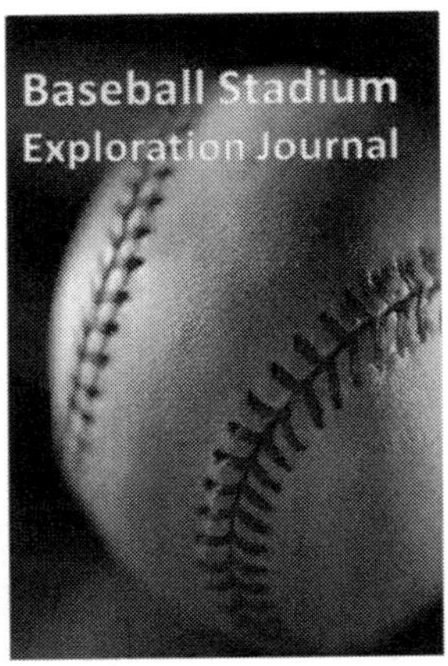

National Parks Exploration Journal

My Bucket List Journal

Lighthouse Exploration Journal

24899617R00050

Printed in Great Britain
by Amazon